10671272

90 AND PROUD OF IT

Copyright © Summersdale Publishers Ltd, 2015

With research by Alistair Cruickshank

All rights reserved.

No part of this book may be reproduced by any means, nor transmitted, nor translated into a machine language, without the written permission of the publishers.

Condition of Sale
This book is sold subject to the condition that it shall not, by way of trade or otherwise, be lent, re-sold, hired out or otherwise circulated in any form of binding or cover other than that in which it is published and without a similar condition including this condition being imposed on the subsequent purchaser.

Summersdale Publishers Ltd
46 West Street
Chichester
West Sussex
PO19 1RP
UK

www.summersdale.com

Printed and bound in the Czech Republic

ISBN: 978-1-84953-694-3

Substantial discounts on bulk quantities of Summersdale books are available to corporations, professional associations and other organisations. For details contact Nicky Douglas by telephone: +44 (0) 1243 756902, fax: +44 (0) 1243 786300 or email: nicky@summersdale.com.

90 AND PROUD OF IT

summersdale

TO.....

FROM.....

CONTENTS

ANOTHER YEAR OLDER.....6

JUST WHAT I ALWAYS WANTED.....29

GRIN AND BEAR IT.....42

DO A LITTLE DANCE, MAKE A LITTLE LOVE...61

YOUNG AT HEART.....77

OLDER AND WISER?.....92

LIVE, LOVE AND LAST.....109

ILLS, PILLS AND TWINGES.....124

CHIN UP, CHEST OUT.....138

ANOTHER YEAR OLDER

YOU ARE NEVER TOO OLD TO SET ANOTHER GOAL OR TO DREAM A NEW DREAM.

C. S. Lewis

I WANT TO LIVE TO BE 120. THAT'S WHEN I WILL START WORRYING ABOUT MY AGE.

Helena Christensen

IF THINGS GET BETTER WITH AGE THEN YOU ARE APPROACHING MAGNIFICENT.

Anonymous

I INTEND TO
LIVE FOREVER,
OR DIE TRYING.

Groucho Marx

LIVE YOUR LIFE AND FORGET YOUR AGE.

Norman Vincent Peale

A BIRTHDAY IS JUST THE FIRST DAY OF ANOTHER 365-DAY JOURNEY AROUND THE SUN. ENJOY THE TRIP.

Anonymous

NO ONE IS SO OLD AS TO THINK THAT HE CANNOT LIVE ONE MORE YEAR.

Cicero

THE OLDER THE FIDDLE, THE SWEETER THE TUNE.

English proverb

YOU CAN'T TURN BACK THE CLOCK, BUT YOU CAN WIND IT UP AGAIN.

Bonnie Prudden

AGE IS SOMETHING THAT DOESN'T MATTER, UNLESS YOU ARE A CHEESE.

Luis Buñuel

YOU CAN LIVE TO BE 100 IF YOU GIVE UP ALL THE THINGS THAT MAKE YOU WANT TO LIVE TO BE 100.

Woody Allen

A TRUE FRIEND REMEMBERS YOUR BIRTHDAY BUT NOT YOUR AGE.

Anonymous

BIRTHDAYS ARE GOOD FOR YOU. STATISTICS SHOW THAT THE PEOPLE WHO HAVE THE MOST LIVE THE LONGEST.

Larry Lorenzoni

FOR ALL THE ADVANCES IN MEDICINE, THERE IS STILL NO CURE FOR THE COMMON BIRTHDAY.

John Glenn

PLEAS'D TO LOOK FORWARD, PLEAS'D TO LOOK BEHIND, AND COUNT EACH BIRTHDAY WITH A GRATEFUL MIND.

Alexander Pope

STOP WORRYING ABOUT THE POTHOLES IN THE ROAD AND CELEBRATE THE JOURNEY!

Anonymous

AS THIS AUSPICIOUS DAY
BEGAN THE RACE
OF EV'RY VIRTUE JOIN'D
WITH EV'RY GRACE;
MAY YOU, WHO OWN THEM,
WELCOME ITS RETURN,
TILL EXCELLENCE, LIKE
YOURS, AGAIN IS BORN.

Francis Jeffrey

I DIDN'T GET OLD ON PURPOSE, IT JUST HAPPENED. IF YOU'RE LUCKY, IT COULD HAPPEN TO YOU.

Andy Rooney

AGE IS JUST A NUMBER. IT'S TOTALLY IRRELEVANT UNLESS, OF COURSE, YOU HAPPEN TO BE A BOTTLE OF WINE.

Joan Collins

THE FIRST 100 YEARS ARE THE HARDEST.

Wilson Mizner

AN OLD-TIMER IS ONE WHO REMEMBERS WHEN WE COUNTED OUR BLESSINGS INSTEAD OF OUR CALORIES.

Anonymous

THE GREAT THING ABOUT GETTING OLDER IS THAT YOU DON'T LOSE ALL THE OTHER AGES YOU'VE BEEN.

Madeleine L'Engle

JUST WHAT I ALWAYS WANTED

YOU KNOW YOU'RE GETTING OLD WHEN THE CANDLES COST MORE THAN THE CAKE.

Bob Hope

YESTERDAY IS HISTORY,
TOMORROW IS A MYSTERY,
BUT TODAY IS A GIFT.
THAT IS WHY IT IS
CALLED THE PRESENT.

Eleanor Roosevelt

IF INSTEAD OF A GEM, OR EVEN A FLOWER, WE SHOULD CAST THE GIFT OF A LOVING THOUGHT INTO THE HEART OF A FRIEND, THAT WOULD BE GIVING AS THE ANGELS GIVE.

George MacDonald

THERE ARE 364 DAYS WHEN YOU MIGHT GET UN-BIRTHDAY PRESENTS... AND ONLY ONE FOR BIRTHDAY PRESENTS, YOU KNOW.

Lewis Carroll

A GIFT WITH A KIND COUNTENANCE IS A DOUBLE PRESENT.

Proverb

NOBODY CAN BE UNCHEERED WITH A BALLOON.

A. A. Milne

SURPRISE IS THE GREATEST GIFT WHICH LIFE CAN GRANT US.

Boris Pasternak

THE MORE CANDLES YOU HAVE ON A CAKE, THE BIGGER THE WISH YOU MAKE.

Anonymous

EACH DAY COMES BEARING ITS OWN GIFTS. UNTIE THE RIBBONS.

Ruth Ann Schabacker

WHY IS A BIRTHDAY CAKE THE ONLY FOOD YOU CAN BLOW ON AND SPIT ON AND EVERYBODY RUSHES TO GET A PIECE?

Bobby Kelton

A HUG IS THE PERFECT GIFT – ONE SIZE FITS ALL AND NOBODY MINDS IF YOU EXCHANGE IT.

Irvin Ball

EVERY BIRTHDAY, EVERY CELEBRATION ENDS WITH SOMETHING SWEET, A CAKE, AND PEOPLE REMEMBER. IT'S ALL ABOUT THE MEMORIES.

Buddy Valastro

GRIN AND BEAR IT

AGEING SEEMS TO BE THE ONLY AVAILABLE WAY TO LIVE A LONG LIFE.

Kitty O'Neill Collins

WHEN IT COMES TO AGE WE'RE ALL IN THE SAME BOAT, ONLY SOME OF US HAVE BEEN ABOARD A LITTLE LONGER.

Leo Probst

OLD MEN ARE FOND OF GIVING GOOD ADVICE, TO CONSOLE THEMSELVES FOR BEING NO LONGER IN A POSITION TO GIVE BAD EXAMPLES.

François de La Rochefoucauld

EVEN IF THERE'S SNOW ON THE ROOF, IT DOESN'T MEAN THE FIRE HAS GONE OUT IN THE FURNACE.

Anonymous

DO NOT WORRY ABOUT AVOIDING TEMPTATION. AS YOU GROW OLDER IT WILL AVOID YOU.

Joey Adams

OLD AGE IS NO PLACE FOR SISSIES.

Bette Davis

I'M LIKE A GOOD CHEESE. I'M JUST GETTING MOULDY ENOUGH TO BE INTERESTING.

Paul Newman

I ADVISE YOU TO GO ON LIVING SOLELY TO ENRAGE THOSE WHO ARE PAYING YOUR ANNUITIES. IT IS THE ONLY PLEASURE I HAVE LEFT.

Oscar Wilde

YOUTH IS A WONDERFUL THING. WHAT A CRIME TO WASTE IT ON CHILDREN.

George Bernard Shaw

I WAS ALWAYS TAUGHT TO RESPECT MY ELDERS AND I'VE NOW REACHED THE AGE WHEN I DON'T HAVE ANYBODY TO RESPECT.

George Burns

GETTING OLD IS A BIT LIKE GETTING DRUNK; EVERYONE ELSE LOOKS BRILLIANT.

Billy Connolly

I STILL HAVE A FULL DECK; I JUST SHUFFLE SLOWER NOW.

Anonymous

AGE IS AN ISSUE OF MIND OVER MATTER. IF YOU DON'T MIND, IT DOESN'T MATTER.

Mark Twain

NO WISE MAN EVER WISHED TO BE YOUNGER.

Jonathan Swift

THE GOOD THING ABOUT BEING OLD IS NOT BEING YOUNG.

Stephen Richards

OLD AGE IS THE MOST UNEXPECTED OF ALL THE THINGS THAT CAN HAPPEN TO A MAN.

Leon Trotsky

OLD AGE IS AN EXCELLENT TIME FOR OUTRAGE. MY GOAL IS TO SAY OR DO AT LEAST ONE OUTRAGEOUS THING EVERY WEEK.

Maggie Kuhn

WHEN I WAS A BOY THE DEAD SEA WAS ONLY SICK.

George Burns

DO A LITTLE DANCE, MAKE A LITTLE LOVE

I CELEBRATE MYSELF,
AND SING MYSELF.

Walt Whitman

YOU ONLY LIVE ONCE,
BUT IF YOU DO IT RIGHT,
ONCE IS ENOUGH.

Mae West

CHERISH ALL YOUR HAPPY MOMENTS: THEY MAKE A FINE CUSHION FOR OLD AGE.

Christopher Morley

ONE OF THE BEST PARTS OF GROWING OLDER? YOU CAN FLIRT ALL YOU LIKE SINCE YOU'VE BECOME HARMLESS.

Liz Smith

LET US CELEBRATE THE OCCASION WITH WINE AND SWEET WORDS.

Plautus

THE OTHER DAY A MAN ASKED ME WHAT I THOUGHT WAS THE BEST TIME OF LIFE. 'WHY,' I ANSWERED WITHOUT A THOUGHT, 'NOW.'

David Grayson

LIFE IS JUST ONE GRAND, SWEET SONG, SO START THE MUSIC.

Ronald Reagan

I ALWAYS MAKE A POINT OF STARTING THE DAY... WITH CHAMPAGNE. IT GOES STRAIGHT TO THE HEART AND CHEERS ONE UP.

John Mortimer

WITH MIRTH AND LAUGHTER LET OLD WRINKLES COME.

William Shakespeare

OLD AGE AND TREACHERY WILL ALWAYS BEAT YOUTH AND EXUBERANCE.

David Mamet

THE OLDER ONE GROWS, THE MORE ONE LIKES INDECENCY.

Virginia Woolf

GROWING OLD IS COMPULSORY — GROWING UP IS OPTIONAL.

Bob Monkhouse

NOBODY LOVES LIFE LIKE HIM THAT'S GROWING OLD.

Sophocles

THE LONGER I LIVE
THE MORE BEAUTIFUL
LIFE BECOMES.

Frank Lloyd Wright

IT'S IMPORTANT TO HAVE A TWINKLE IN YOUR WRINKLE.

Anonymous

YOUNG AT HEART

THE GREAT SECRET THAT ALL OLD PEOPLE SHARE IS THAT YOU REALLY HAVEN'T CHANGED... YOUR BODY CHANGES, BUT YOU DON'T CHANGE AT ALL.

Doris Lessing

TO KEEP THE HEART UNWRINKLED, TO BE HOPEFUL, KINDLY, CHEERFUL, REVERENT – THAT IS TO TRIUMPH OVER OLD AGE.

Thomas B. Aldrich

OLD AGE IS NOT JUST FOR GROWN-UPS.

Benny Bellamacina

WHITE HAIR OFTEN COVERS THE HEAD, BUT THE HEART THAT HOLDS IT IS EVER YOUNG.

Honoré de Balzac

YOUTH WOULD BE AN IDEAL STATE IF IT CAME A LITTLE LATER IN LIFE.

H. H. Asquith

THE IMPORTANT THING... IS NOT HOW MANY YEARS IN YOUR LIFE, BUT HOW MUCH LIFE IN YOUR YEARS!

Edward Stieglitz

TO WIN BACK MY YOUTH... THERE IS NOTHING I WOULDN'T DO – EXCEPT TAKE EXERCISE, GET UP EARLY, OR BE A USEFUL MEMBER OF THE COMMUNITY.

Oscar Wilde

AGE DOES NOT DIMINISH THE EXTREME DISAPPOINTMENT OF HAVING A SCOOP OF ICE CREAM FALL FROM THE CONE.

Jim Fiebig

INSIDE EVERY OLDER PERSON IS A YOUNGER PERSON – WONDERING WHAT THE HELL HAPPENED.

Cora Harvey Armstrong

YOU'RE ONLY AS YOUNG AS THE LAST TIME YOU CHANGED YOUR MIND.

Timothy Leary

OLD AGE IS LIKE EVERYTHING ELSE. TO MAKE A SUCCESS OF IT, YOU'VE GOT TO START YOUNG.

Theodore Roosevelt

THE SECRET TO STAYING YOUNG IS TO LIVE HONESTLY, EAT SLOWLY, AND LIE ABOUT YOUR AGE.

Lucille Ball

EVERYONE IS THE AGE OF THEIR HEART.

Guatemalan proverb

IT TAKES A LONG TIME TO BECOME YOUNG.

Pablo Picasso

OLDER AND WISER?

WHEN YOU GET RID OF ALL THE OLDER PEOPLE, YOU GET RID OF ALL THE WISDOM.

Terraine Francois

KEEP THE ENTHUSIASM OF YOUR YOUTH AND TREASURE THE WISDOM OF OLD AGE.

Lailah Gifty Akita

NOW THAT I'M 91, AS OPPOSED TO BEING 90, I'M MUCH WISER.

Betty White

WISDOM DOESN'T NECESSARILY COME WITH AGE. SOMETIMES AGE JUST SHOWS UP ALL BY ITSELF.

Tom Wilson

THE YOUNG SOW WILD OATS. THE OLD GROW SAGE.

Winston Churchill

I'M NOT YOUNG ENOUGH TO KNOW EVERYTHING.

J. M. Barrie

THE MORE SAND HAS ESCAPED FROM THE HOURGLASS OF OUR LIFE, THE CLEARER WE SHOULD SEE THROUGH IT.

Jean Paul

IF I HAD MY LIFE TO LIVE OVER AGAIN, I'D MAKE THE SAME MISTAKES, ONLY SOONER.

Tallulah Bankhead

AS YOU GROW OLDER, YOU LEARN TO UNDERSTAND LIFE A LITTLE BETTER.

Solomon Burke

ALL LIFE IS AN EXPERIMENT. THE MORE EXPERIMENTS YOU MAKE THE BETTER.

Ralph Waldo Emerson

IF YOU CAN SPEND A PERFECTLY USELESS AFTERNOON IN A PERFECTLY USELESS MANNER, YOU HAVE LEARNED HOW TO LIVE.

Lin Yutang

TO KNOW HOW TO GROW OLD IS THE MASTERWORK OF WISDOM, AND ONE OF THE MOST DIFFICULT CHAPTERS IN THE GREAT ART OF LIVING.

Henri-Frédéric Amiel

THEY TOLD ME IF I GOT OLDER I'D GET WISER. IN THAT CASE I MUST BE A GENIUS.

George Burns

IT'S WHAT YOU LEARN AFTER YOU KNOW IT ALL THAT COUNTS.

John Wooden

NO MAN IS EVER OLD ENOUGH TO KNOW BETTER.

Holbrook Jackson

AS ONE GROWS OLDER, ONE BECOMES WISER AND MORE FOOLISH.

François de La Rochefoucauld

LIVE, LOVE AND LAST

IF I'D KNOWN I WAS GOING TO LIVE THIS LONG, I'D HAVE TAKEN BETTER CARE OF MYSELF.

Eubie Blake

YOUTH DISSERVES;
MIDDLE AGE CONSERVES;
OLD AGE PRESERVES.

Martin H. Fischer

YOU CAN'T HELP GETTING OLDER, BUT YOU DON'T HAVE TO GET OLD.

George Burns

THERE IS NO OLD AGE. THERE IS, AS THERE ALWAYS WAS, JUST YOU.

Carol Matthau

THE GOOD OLD DAYS ARE NOW.

Tom Clancy

OLD PEOPLE AREN'T EXEMPT FROM HAVING FUN AND DANCING.

Liz Smith

THE ABILITY TO LAUGH, ESPECIALLY AT OURSELVES, KEEPS THE HEART LIGHT AND THE MIND YOUNG.

Anonymous

A COMFORTABLE OLD AGE IS THE REWARD OF A WELL-SPENT YOUTH.

Maurice Chevalier

AGE, LIKE DISTANCE,
LENDS A DOUBLE CHARM.

Oliver Wendell Holmes Jr

FEW THINGS ARE MORE DELIGHTFUL THAN GRANDCHILDREN FIGHTING OVER YOUR LAP.

Doug Larson

I LOVE EVERYTHING THAT'S OLD: OLD FRIENDS, OLD TIMES, OLD MANNERS, OLD BOOKS, OLD WINE.

Oliver Goldsmith

HE WHO LAUGHS, LASTS!

Mary Pettibone Poole

MY ADVICE FOR LIFE: DANCE AND SING YOUR SONG WHILE THE PARTY IS STILL ON.

Rasheed Ogunlaru

HE DRANK TO LIFE, TO ALL IT HAD BEEN, TO WHAT IT WAS, TO WHAT IT WOULD BE.

Sean O'Casey

ILLS, PILLS AND TWINGES

AS YOU GET OLDER THREE THINGS HAPPEN. THE FIRST IS YOUR MEMORY GOES, AND I CAN'T REMEMBER THE OTHER TWO...

Norman Wisdom

IF WRINKLES MUST BE WRITTEN UPON OUR BROWS, LET THEM NOT BE WRITTEN UPON THE HEART. THE SPIRIT SHOULD NEVER GROW OLD.

James A. Garfield

I DON'T FEEL OLD. I DON'T FEEL ANYTHING TILL NOON. THAT'S WHEN IT'S TIME FOR MY NAP.

Bob Hope

OLDER PEOPLE SHOULDN'T EAT HEALTH FOOD, THEY NEED ALL THE PRESERVATIVES THEY CAN GET.

Robert Orben

WRINKLES SHOULD MERELY INDICATE WHERE THE SMILES HAVE BEEN.

Mark Twain

I DON'T NEED YOU TO REMIND ME OF MY AGE. I HAVE A BLADDER TO DO THAT FOR ME.

Stephen Fry

I'LL KEEP SWIVELLING MY HIPS UNTIL THEY NEED REPLACING.

Tom Jones

THE EASIEST WAY TO DIMINISH THE APPEARANCE OF WRINKLES IS TO KEEP YOUR GLASSES OFF WHEN YOU LOOK IN THE MIRROR.

Joan Rivers

DON'T LET AGEING GET YOU DOWN. IT'S TOO HARD TO GET BACK UP.

John Wagner

AGE SELDOM ARRIVES SMOOTHLY OR QUICKLY. IT'S MORE OFTEN A SUCCESSION OF JERKS.

Jean Rhys

YEARS MAY WRINKLE THE SKIN, BUT TO GIVE UP ENTHUSIASM WRINKLES THE SOUL.

Samuel Ullman

LAUGHTER DOESN'T REQUIRE TEETH.

Bill Newton

DON'T RETOUCH MY WRINKLES... I WOULD NOT WANT IT TO BE THOUGHT THAT I HAD LIVED FOR ALL THESE YEARS WITHOUT SOMETHING TO SHOW FOR IT.

Queen Elizabeth, The Queen Mother

CHIN UP, CHEST OUT

I'M NOT SURE THAT OLD AGE ISN'T THE BEST PART OF LIFE.

C. S. Lewis

WHEN GRACE IS JOINED WITH WRINKLES, IT IS ADORABLE. THERE IS AN UNSPEAKABLE DAWN IN HAPPY OLD AGE.

Victor Hugo

YOUTH IS THE GIFT OF NATURE, BUT AGE IS A WORK OF ART.

Garson Kanin

I'M LIKE OLD WINE. THEY DON'T BRING ME OUT VERY OFTEN, BUT I'M WELL PRESERVED.

Rose Kennedy

TIME IS A DRESSMAKER SPECIALISING IN ALTERATIONS.

Faith Baldwin

WE TURN NOT
OLDER WITH YEARS,
BUT NEWER EVERY DAY.

Emily Dickinson

OLD AGE: THE CROWN OF LIFE.

Cicero

MY IDEA OF HELL IS TO BE YOUNG AGAIN.

Marge Piercy

BECAUSE OF YOUR SMILE, YOU MAKE LIFE MORE BEAUTIFUL.

Thích Nhât Hạnh

IT'S NOT HOW OLD YOU ARE, BUT HOW YOU ARE OLD.

Marie Dressler

OUR WRINKLES ARE OUR MEDALS OF THE PASSAGE OF LIFE.

Lauren Hutton

PERHAPS ONE HAS TO BE VERY OLD BEFORE ONE LEARNS HOW TO BE AMUSED RATHER THAN SHOCKED.

Pearl S. Buck

IF YOU SURVIVE LONG ENOUGH, YOU'RE REVERED – RATHER LIKE AN OLD BUILDING.

Katharine Hepburn

THE MORE YOU PRAISE AND CELEBRATE YOUR LIFE, THE MORE THERE IS IN LIFE TO CELEBRATE.

Oprah Winfrey

IN OUR DREAMS WE ARE ALWAYS YOUNG.

Sarah Louise Delany

WE ARE NOT LIMITED BY OUR OLD AGE; WE ARE LIBERATED BY IT.

Stu Mittleman

MAY YOU LIVE ALL THE DAYS OF YOUR LIFE.

Jonathan Swift

THE ELDERLY DON'T DRIVE THAT BADLY; THEY'RE JUST THE ONLY ONES WITH TIME TO DO THE SPEED LIMIT.

Jason Love

IT IS TRUE YOU ARE GENTLY SHOULDERED OFF THE STAGE, BUT THEN YOU ARE GIVEN SUCH A COMFORTABLE FRONT STALL AS SPECTATOR.

Jane Harrison on old age

OLD AGE HAS ITS PLEASURES WHICH, THOUGH DIFFERENT, ARE NOT LESS THAN THE PLEASURES OF YOUTH.

W. Somerset Maugham

YOU DON'T GET OLDER,
YOU GET BETTER.

Shirley Bassey

Meet Esme!

Our feathered friend Esme loves finding perfect quotes for the perfect occasion, and is almost as good at collecting them as she is at collecting twigs for her nest. She's always full of joy and happiness, singing her messages of goodwill in this series of uplifting, heart-warming books.

Follow Esme on Twitter at **@EsmeTheBird**.

For more information about our books, find us on Facebook at **Summersdale Publishers** and follow us on Twitter at **@Summersdale**.

www.summersdale.com